# Passive Income: Make Your Passion A Passive Income

By

## Sarah Bailey

Copyright © 2017

http://zorbobook.org/passive/passprint.html

zorbobook.org

# INTRODUCTION

The purpose of this book: Have you ever wanted to make a living utilizing just your passion alone? Are you sick and tired of the fat cat rat race? Are you more interested in the things you want to do and less of the things that you HAVE to do for someone else, eight hours a day, six days a week? Are you looking to just replace your income, take a vacation or just sit at home, reading a book, while your bank account counts cash deposits by customers using your website like an ATM? Ask yourself, how much money would it cost to buy an ATM machine to dispense your passion as you get paid at the same time? How much would that be worth to you?

This book is less about propensity and more about product leadership, information delivery and self-absorption all reasons to make way for a better life. By consuming gobs of information as key to the first step of learning to become your own boss, this my friend- is key to your success. Knowledge, information, strategy, delivery and promotion. Inside are find three books where each delivers, imaginative knowledge, information and strategy as one single book. This is a unique and powerful book, using a form of delivery in a series called "Close Your Eyes", and imagined. This book is in your hands. It is a powerful book. You can take the information and apply it. You could simply digest the process as entertaining information. The choice is yours.

The benefits of reading this book are enormous.

You are not obligated to re-influence your mind, or get busy doing the things you need to do to build an income ATM machine based upon your passion.

But watch out, this book is an interesting read. There are no facts, no figures, just pure information for anyone looking a new perspective to passive income.

# THE WOW FACTOR

Hey, before you continue reading this book, can I interest you in a *free book* that I wrote that teaches you how to earn more money using your computer, a website, a squeeze page, a $5 source of traffic to start your website traffic engine, plus I teach you how to pump up an unlimited google supply of free perpetual traffic and much, much more.

On top of all that, I show you in a few videos? Right now you can get a *FREE* copy, my weekly newsletter but you have to act now!

Click here for instant access!

http://zorbobook.org/passive/passprint.html

Hey, one last thing?
We email **ONCE PER WEEK and DO NOT SPAM**.

### OTHER BOOK TITLES

LIST BUILDING: ALL IN ONE CRAZY TRICK LIST BUILD SECRETS FOR ADVANCED

How to Write Persuasive Emails: the 10 Minute Guide To Writing Persuasive eMail That Sell

List Building: All-In-One Solution Crazy Trick List Building Secrets For Beginners

The Self Taught Programmer: Illustrated FTP Batch Programming Scripting

# TABLE OF CONTENTS

## Book ONE

For the past three months I have had nothing but a great deal of fun writing books for you to read and enjoy. I am very flattered by the people who have downloaded and read my work, thus far.

This book single book is actually three books bundled into one enormous book. Just like my other books, you do not need to have a lot of money to get started.

You need only the will to listen, the desire to take action and the strength to fight self-doubt. Everyone is a winner and more importantly, so are YOU!

Here is what most book do that people dislike:

-Obligate you to take action

-Force you to be independent

-Trash your friends

-Kill your social life

-Force you to attack self doubt

-Cause you hate and discontent

-Create worry and regret

-Throw away their book or give it away

There will be none of that with my books. It is easier to entice than to enforce. The objective of the "Close your eyes series" which is bundled here into one large book, is to explain, demonstrate and teach. This is not, the be all, end all book.

The year 2017 is the best year ever to implement change. There is nothing more and nothing less in this unusual book where we discuss and provide a solution.

I hope that this book will educate, enlighten and entertain you as you to discover our passive income.

# CHAPTER 1 - CLOSE MY

Today is December 31, 2017. For a few weeks, I have been theorizing about how exciting 2017 will be. Today will be the first day to put those thought on paper to share with the whole world, good, bad or maybe indifferent.

The premise of the "Close My Eyes" series is to prepare readers for the brewing financial euphoria that will come across America again like a wave in the year 2017.

If you will recall, in the last 80's prices begin to rise, wages began to tick up and a huge generation of new opportunities begin to emerge. It was exciting and everyone was happy. Gosh, the stock market started to climb and new opportunities- wow.

No one could for see how tiny indicators when put together would form the perfect storm.

Now, I must admit with every upturn, there is a down turn and from what we all recollect, the creative ideas of some of the best minds, took bad mortgages and mixed them into new mortgages generating clean securities that were bought and sold like milk at the grocery store.  Toast and jelly was being sold like hot cakes and everybody was happy. In California, you could buy a house for like nothing and sell it like it was the next best thing to apple pie. I know because I was a part of it. I saw the roller-coaster, no I was on the roller-coaster all the way till the end.

The winners walked away wealthy and the losers should have never been able to buy properties to begin with. Now this is just my small bubble of a take on the situation, but I will be the first to tell you I am not a financial genius.

I am not a writer either, but as an indie publisher, I have a message and this book is my plat form. Here is my famous quote from a YouTube sensation.

I want to convince you that two plus two equals five. But you know that two plus two equals four. But if I spend enough time, I can convince you that two plus to equals five.

This phrase comes from a famous YouTube, personality that sells an indie publishing course.

# CHAPTER 2 – GETTING STARTED

Let me say, by no means am I a finical genius. I am not an accountant, but what I plan to help you do is to change your mind set. I want to change your mind set in such a small way, that later you will want to try other chess moves of your life, that will add up to a different take on how you perceive your financial situation.

Please, take a minute and imagine this. Close your eyes. Do it.

Close your eyes and imagine what it would be like if you were driving a better car than the one you have in your drive way or apartment parking lot? What would does that feel like? What would be your concerns? What would be your worries? Can you make your car note payment? Is the car nicer than your current car? Of course the car would be nicer. We are simply using our imagination and there is nothing wrong with that.

The biggest problem with people today when it comes to moving forward, becoming successful in some way, shape or form in YOUR life is changing YOUR mindset.

Think about it. As a publisher or author it is very easy to delegate this job to someone else. That person might be a professional writer, or someone who desires to utilize their talent to write what you desire them to write about.

Making the decision to have your book idea written by someone else other than yourself is simplistic. Gosh, anyone can do that.

Yes, please open your eyes. Everyday week or two weeks or so, we all receive a paycheck. With that paycheck we pay our bills. A portion is utilized for this, and a portion of utilized for that. But what we truly want when it comes to our finances is finical independence. We all want more money, we all want more freedom, but where we lack in our lives is taking steps. Taking the necessary steps to creating the mind set necessary to become, a new independent business person. What we lack is another person just like YOU. A-you- that is doing this part of the work. The reading, the learning and the generating income part.

# CHAPTER 3 – LIVING IN THREE HOUSES

Everyone has bills. Everyone has credit card. Everyone has many, many, many financial obligations. But when asked, how many savings accounts you own, the answer will likely yield in high probability of all cases is one account. Now, there will be a few of you who have zero accounts. Nothing wrong with that.

Most people who have lived on this earth for more than thirty years, will most likely have two or more credit cards.

As a matter of fact, if you counted the number of cards you could use as a credit card, that number would likely increase. The truth of the matter is, a finical wave is about to hit every American living in the United States and this new 2017 wave will finally be an opportunity for those with a changed mind set to take advantage of opportunities that make perfect since.

But to be in a position to ride the wave as opposed to being under the wave, will take changing your mind set. Changing the way that you think. Taking a chance like betting on stocks that will rise and fall at your will. Now, this is what I ask that you do.

Close your eyes. Now imagine driving your car in your neighborhood or riding the bus, count the number of banks in your neighborhood. How many banks do you see in your mind's eye? In my neighborhood, there are so many banks that, at every gas station- you see the bank.

Now count them. Count the number of banks that you see in your 3rd eye.

Do you see three banks within walking distance of each other? Do you see five banks within walking distance? Now, may I ask how many banks do you bank with? If the answer is one bank, please "Open your eyes". If the answer is three banks, please "Open your eyes."

Thank you. Now you can open your eyes for the folks who failed to open their eyes.

Moving forward, I stated that 2017 will yield a financial wave? I told you that what I am about to describe to you will most likely become a bankers dream. What I am about to ask that you do is consider opening a second savings account, depositing the minimum requirement. That's all I ask.

But what I have failed to tell you is the why and the, what the heck is in it for YOU? By the way, I do not work for any bank. I do not endorse any bank and I do not render financial consideration in stocks, bonds, etc. The information served here is for informational purposes- I say these things to be sure to cover my legal representations here. Gosh, it does not make since not TO open a savings account for what YOU are about to do and as such, the ramifications for doing so keeps you responsible and of course, we want to see progress and not money manipulation or contamination.

I told you from the beginning that I am not a financial wizard. But what I will tell you is that, by opening a second and a third saving account meeting the minimum requirements will put you on the road to building an income.

What I have just described to you is by no means crazy, because the objective for those with no will power, no DOIT attitude or personality might likely try taking a baby step toward riding the 2017 financial wave. Does that make sense?

Baby steps.

The DOIT motivational phrase may or may not cut it with you or society today. We don't just DOIT anymore with as many distractions as there are today. We all want the results of just DOIT but the reality is, DOIT just does not work anymore.

Today, we have this understanding that DOIT does not work and having someone else do it for us is just as bad, that if it were "that easy", everyone would be just DOING IT.

Let me introduce an entirely new, realistic way to changing your mindset.

I am going to ask that you do something that will make banks happy, you happy and at the same time, provide you with options and opportunity all at the same time. Open your eyes. I'm sorry, I never asked you to close your eyes. Closing your eyes is very important and it's an easy exercise. I apologize.

# CHAPTER 4 – WOW, WHAT A FEELING

Close your eyes please.

As ridiculous as my asking you to open a savings account utilizing whatever funds that you have with meeting the minimum requirements, might not float your boat.

For some people who have only one savings and checking account, let's ask this question. When the money or funds from either account is gone, where do you draw upon for more funds when any emergency arises? Is there a rainy day account somewhere in the name of a friend? Maybe, you still draw upon those people whom we call mom and dad? No matter what the case, here it is- by opening a second and third saving account within a walking distance of banks as I am going to suggest, will give you wow what a feeling.

Yes. Please open a savings account close to your home and within walking distance or on a route close to your way home.

Why on earth would it be a good idea to follow this ridicules advice or suggestion? How in the world is opening a savings account with what few funds you may or may not already have will put YOU in a situation where 2017 will blow your mind. The answer my friend is not in this book. The answer to this question continues, so please read on.

The word income has always confused me? I come from an environment of savings, but I have never ever had money for which to save until a few years ago, when I worked for a bank.

Banks hate people btw. Hate is a strong word. Banks hate people.

They hey the people who take advantage of them for not using them for which or what they were built and designed for.

Banks are in the business of what? Helping you solve your problem. Now, most people go to banks for money troubles. Few, if any rational person ever goes to the bank seeking a solution for solving an emotional problem, but they do exists. Have you ever see a person cry because they have too much money? Then you need to work at a bank. And yes, there are people who cry about having too much money because they do not know what to do with the money. It happens every day.

While I would love to provide an example, the purpose here is not to overly demonstrate wealth. Gosh, the idea here is to ask that you open an account.

The objective here is to ALSO, gush about the process of opening an account.

Close your eyes please. With your eyes closed, you select a bank. Any bank that may be within walking distances of your current bank or you may have found two or more banks together within a few feet of each other. The idea here is to examine together what you have to do to open an account.

The most obvious thing you must do is walk into the bank. Upon doing, your eyes are most likely looking around inside the bank, because it is new to you. You are looking for assistance. Your objective is the new accounts person. You may have to wait for a few minutes, thereby taking a seat and for good reason.

You may also want to take advantage of the coffee, tea, cookies and depending on the month, Danishes or other delights including candy, which may be within a few inches of everything else that's described here.

Explore, the feelings of being in a new environment, being waited upon and truly made welcome to the bank of your choice with the objective of opening a savings account. It's exciting. I ask that you savor the moment and open your eyes.

I have done something that no one, including all of the motivational speakers you will ever hear or have heard of. You have opened a second or third savings account with your mind. You have read on these pages a glimpse of good feelings. You have successfully programmed yourself, changed your mindset and you've walked with me, and I with you. We've both visited the bank. Yahoo!

# CHAPTER 5 – THE REVIEW

Over the course of a few minutes, I may have convinced you to shape or change your mind differently.

I may have even convinced you to perform the simple task of opening one savings account. As I have stated and will continue to state so, I am not a financial genius, nor do I claim to be one. As a matter of fact, if I were to endorse a single financial instrument it would probably explode beyond everyone's ability to afford it. I would ask that you consider participation in purchasing the "Franklin California Tax Free Mutual Fund."

I would purchase this instruments and recommend it whole hardily, because of my experience of how this instrument saved me for its worth. The trouble for all readers is, you must live in California to appreciate the no state or federal tax.

In this book I have asked that you perform, a small task. The asking and providing you with, as little information in this case as the eventual magnitude as to how 2017 will become the influencer of the financial wave that is approaching. I wanted to make a clear comparison about feel good books that motivate you with logic and how the approach to modification and action is reasonable.

The most powerful position that any human can be in when our faced with making a financial decision is the ability to make a choice.

When I go to a burger place and I sit down, I am presented with a menu. From the menu, I select those items in the form of a choice or selection.

The more choices you have in making a financial decision, the better you will feel and the more serious you will be about making the right choice.

The objective is to make a decision. To choose, an option that will change your financial condition.

There are lots and lots of feel good books you can read. Most of them provide excellent advice. Yet, many of those feel good books prepare or cause inaction.

This is not a feel good book. This is a take action book, and if you are still up for this ride- then read on.

## Book TWO - The Message

Writing a book is very hard work. There is no right, there is no wrong. There is only guessing and no matter how well you plan or implement, market and all of the other stuff that goes into publishing, the biggest boost that you can give to yourself as an indie is software that bends to your will and that enables you to write faster, publish quickly and best organize YOU.

Like every indie publisher, I do expect every book I write to be that game changer, but folks- every book will not reach that kind of success.

But what I can do is earn just a little income by using and encouraging those potential writers interested in doing what I do here, to purchase products I use.

Products that truly does all of the things necessary to be and to become successful. The product for which I a endorsing for which I receive a small commission when you purchase is called KD Publishing System.

Let me be clear again, I do receive a commission when you purchase through my link and when you do so, it is very much appreciated.

There are many systems out there that you can utilize but for the money and for its ability for this author to quickly and easily create a publishing empire, KD Publishing System works unlike anything I have seen out there for such a very small investment.

# CHAPTER 1 –PRODUCT SOLUTION

The best product I ever thought up was my first book, Dear Microsoft. I wrote this book in one day, because I truly felt that the Windows operating system on a new computer should be just as fast as the previous operating system. Let me define new. Brand new store bought machines.

Most people would agree with me, and there were certainly those who believed my book was just something that would sit on a book shelf, all alone.

To my surprise, it was a master piece. The next book that I wrote thereafter was Dear Dell. The premise was not the same and like everyone else, I have ideas and thoughts about their product, that I wanted Dell to learn about.

But just the same, I created a good product. It was so, good that I quickly became aware of the grave responsibility I have as an indie publisher. I have to speak my mind, stand up for my belief[s and entertain and educate my readers, my customer and my fans.

I quickly followed the YouTube sensation and agree that social media and paid advertising is not the proper way to promote my product.

The best way, would be to make sure I select money keywords. I also needed to have a great book cover and concentrate on reviews, working with the Amazon search engine and my umbrella of keywords for success.

Understanding this symmetry, it became very clear that writing an ebook fell directly into the path and philosophy of generating income based on this idea which I announce to YOU!

Take advantage of the financial wave that is brewing off shore. It's coming, and it's coming fast. Did you know that audio is being consumed faster than digital print, with paper printing being second as opposed to third?

# CHAPTER 2 – DEVELOPING A PLATFORM

eBook publishing is very hard work. eBook publishing rules and regulations by the YouTube sensation puts the process in the hands of the young publisher square on.

The process is very easy, but very, very hard. You can either write the books yourself, or you can outsource your book. Additionally, there are other very interesting techniques you can utilize to write eBook very, very quickly.

There are many, many courses on the subject of eBook creation and building a passive business. But the most shocking problem found is that everyone tells a similar story, but only the best will show social proof that they are actually making money.

Some leaders will ask that you to invest in social media, which my YouTube sensation will tell you is ludicrous and it does not work, and there are some guru's that will tell you to utilize PPC, PTC and other promotional ventures that require you to spend x dollars out of pocket, only to discoverer they don't work and he tells you why.

But more importantly, when the kindle code has been cracked, there is nothing but good to say about the real success and effort put forth to become successful at building a successful passive income.

The tools necessary to build a passive income may already be in your current prevue. A word processor program, a kindle account, the desire and know how to create a cover and a system for finding profitable keywords, along with a method for organizing the madness.

Publishing an ebook, I repeat is very, very hard. But it can be made very easy when you outsource a lot of the work, build a process or system. Perform everything in a step by step process.

For anyone building a passive income, writing one book per week and learning the trade as time permits in very realistic.

A few suggestions would be to locate a mentor on YouTube. Follow a few mentors and be sure to take an offered free ebook course.

But more importantly would be to make sure your story is heard as it could be invaluable to the world and those around you.

Writing is about making money, but when you have a message to give to the world, then the money sometimes comes second and naturally.

Think about your story and get it on paper. There is this myth, that there is nothing that people don't want to read about YOU that is a secret. Truth be told, the secret is what people are mostly interested in.

The secret to passive income for example. There is a secret and there is a magic formula. But honestly, like publishing- there is a lot of parts to the engine. So, if you are still interested and I'm sure you are. Let's show you more of the pieces to a passive income.

# CHAPTER 3 – SHORT READS

Upon setting up a saving account, the objective is also registering this SAVINGs account with a PayPal account.

Caution: You will also need a Kindle publishing account. Got one? Great.

The process is very simple. Using your second savings account, you like your Kindle account with your PayPal account. When you are paid by Kindle, the money will show up in this account.

A common question is why not utilize an already established banking account. The answer is two-fold.

Accountability and accessibility. Besides, I trust you, it's the devil inside I don't trust.

Building a passive income means that money is deposited into your account like an ATM, where the funds are counted and accounted for.

There is no accountability if the money put into the account is spent and of course, at the end of the year you will have to account for the taxes to both state and federal that will have to be accounted for.

I am by no means an accountant. Nor am I qualified to give financial advice, but it certainly would be in your best interest to allow the account to grow through your efforts of one year and at the end of the year, settle your debt and parcel the funds as you see fit.

After successfully turning this account into an ATM from the start, doubling your efforts might entail putting funds into your third saving account from the second part of publishing.

The first part of publishing is Kindle, but the second part of publishing is books in print. To do so, you will need a smash words account and lastly, the final piece would be utilizing an audiobook service. Where you book will be bought and sold to customers interested in listening to your book.

Now, I'm sure everyone by now is wonder, where is this going and what will YOU be doing. Like everyone else making money hand over fist, someone has to spend it. Right?

Kindle is not the only platform for selling your ideas in print. There are many, many other platforms you can sign up for and most of them are free and help you in many, many ways. The decision to use another platform is yours. You are not obligated to use Kindle. You could however, setup your own platform. It will NOT be as easy to use or has a big brand name, but with PayPal or Gum road, you can easily collect the RAIN.

Take a powder and read on please.

# CHAPTER 4 – PUTTING IT ALL TOGETHER

Close your eyes. "Imagine for one moment that 2017 became for you, the financial windfall you desired or had desired for a very, very long time.

Don't laugh. It's true! It can happen and it will happen for you. You started when you read this book. 2017 will be the year for you. Now, understand as I continue.

Your dreams have come true and you are no long afraid to fail. Your ability to take risks is reasonably acceptable and you are not afraid of failure. You have built your financial goals based on a solid foundation." You can open your eyes now.

Are you ready to purchase a domain name to sell your own brand of eBooks for a much higher price than what you could sell on Amazon, but these books are longer and much more valuable and highly sought after by your following.

Of course you are.

On that premise, it is time to purchase a domain name and hosting. Another product you might want to invest in is either an autoresponder or a platform to broadcast your message at one time to all of your paying customers, with the objective of getting a 12% response to your shout out prospects and customers to purchase another new product you would like to promote.

The product is one that YOU created, or one that is already selling, yet popular.

If your mailing lists was say, 1,200 addresses and 10% responded, to a $45 dollar product promotion.

Your return or income would be over "lots of money" in sales for just a single shout. If your shout was weekly, your income would be over "lots of money" a month.

While the number here are all hypothetical based on a low response rate, the objective and YOUR subsequent reactions would be the same. You would make bank on sales.

## Book THREE

I would like to thank you for buying my book. You have reached the best part of my book. Most people understand the processes of making money, but for those of us who are new at this, we have a long ways to go. Now, I need to warn you about perfection and control. Both are necessary for the creation of a product or service. But what can hold you back is the perfection part of being in business.

Not everything is mirror image perfect and when you try to mirror image your product to perfection, you never get started. You never get past the finish line.

Let's talk about control. Not only do you need to let go of certain things, understand that you are not perfect in those areas. If you such at math, then why are you performing the process of completing your taxes. You will simply have to have to redone all over again, so let someone else do this stuff ok.

In this last book I try my best to wrap up the process by showing you how to build an ATM machine, YOUR way. I provide the information, but it is up to YOU to fill up the machine and decide the direction. Along the way, your journey will thrill and excite you.

Understand that you are by no means obligated to do anything here. The success here, is not measured by the number of people who follow through to change, improve or switch directions towards retirement. The success here for anyone reading this book is completing the entire book with a thirst for more knowledge. The knowledge acquired with the intent behind it, requires not just one course, class or lecture, but many, many, many more as a jumping stone to taking action.

# CHAPTER 1 – THE NINJA MIND

Every New Year, everyone over 30 talks about their new year's resolution. The number one issue placed on their list is weight loss.

The success of achieving the goal is few and far between. I love that phrase. What that means is, the weight loss in pounds will not be lost.

Then why suggest losing weight in the first place? Well, for starters, we all want to look better. We all want to look sexy. We all want that look!

BUT the reality is, perception is the reality. What you do and what you say fall into the category of getting your ass off the couch and going to the gym. Well, the likelihood of you getting off the couch and following up and going to the gym is not going to happen. First off, you need a gym membership and you need all the things that entail working out. So folks, what is this thing about weight all about?

Folks, this chapter is not about weight loss. Far from it, this chapter is about saying and doing. In my last book, I asked you to open a savings account. I failed to tell you why, but if you did open an account, you have just changed your financial positon. You now have choices. This is something that you did not have before. But today, when you drive past that very same bank you can now look at the building with a different attitude. You can say, I have an account with that bank. I am a customer of that bank. And finally, when you have opened or acquired several accounts with different banks your perspective of weight loss is a whole lot different. You are in a different league.

This book again, is not about losing weight. This book is not about what you believe and cannot change or do. What this book is about is talking a look to see the real you. Are you ready for you?

Are you ready to change your mind? Well, for now- the answer is no. But after reading just a few more chapters, maybe this book will change your mind. Maybe in just a few more sentences not only will you be open to something new and different, but maybe you might just learn a little bit more about what this book is really about.

# CHAPTER 2 – WHAT IS THE 2017 PARADIGM SHIFT?

Everyone has very good intentions. But intentions do not always equate to good decisions or the act of doing something good. When I was growing up, I was never taught the world of business. As a matter of fact, I believe you will agree that business is the act of buying and selling. There are some good deal, and some bad deal.

You can spot a good purchase or a bad purchase, but what about today. What about right now. Can you spot a good book vs a book that's going to take something from you? Well, in a sense no. As a matter of fact, this book is not going to take from you, but rather give you what you need to know. The world out there is changing and today, as opposed to tomorrow- you are going to take something from it. You are going to take your fair share of success. Now, do me this one favor.

Close your eyes. Imagine getting your ass out of bed and going to work. You perform xyz task for axy company. Over the course of a few days, you have given a total of 30 hours or more of YOUR time. In return, you receive money for your efforts in the form of a paycheck.

For most people, that paycheck has some form of taxes subtracted from it. The reality is, you do not produce something that works 24/7. In the end, you have not created a tangible product that now generates an income for you. Then, I say get one. That's right. Get another income producing asset that works for you. Now, I'm not saying go out and get another job where YOU work another 4 to 6 hours part time. What I am saying is you need another you. Now, not to be stupid here, but one of us already work and spend the money we make already. You don't need another you in that context. What you need is another YOU who will work their ass off and not complain, not get tried or quit. You need a, YOU who is working 24/7 and doing the do. You need what's called an income generator. It is so easy to complain about not having money when in fact what you truly need is money working for you.

But get this, money is not an asset like an ever green product. Let me see. Let's take for example this book. This book is a tangible asset. It works for me, making money. It does so, by educating you and providing you with the information you need to be successful in this area of your life if and when YOU choose. But for me what this book represents is a store. It's a store of information that I create once. But this store, is sold many times over.

So, the bottom line is you need a something that generates a passive income. Something that is an expression of you, a product or a service that people would want to buy. Are you a rock star? Can you sing? Do you dance? If you can't do any of these things, then what can you do? Can you write a book/ Can you cook a meal that is so good, people want and desire what you can deliver? Maybe you are a leader of men. Maybe you can provide people with insight into the future? There may be a gift somewhere inside you that "can work" that people desire that can generate an income. I really don't' know but the point here is to demonstrate that YOU have something. Just discover what that SOMETHING is.

Now open your eyes. 2017 is the year of the Paradigm Shift. This is a shift where those who are aware or knowledgeable of the incoming financial windfall can take advantage of this wave, or for those not listening, watching or wondering; the gust of prosperity will pass by and once gone, there is very little you can do.

Profit is the difference between all of the associated costs involved in creating the product minus expenses. Now, I am not a financial wizard of anything of that nature.

But what I am trying to get across to you is, today our society has people who count pennies and depend on this formula. These people are not counting the big differences between the dollars and the hundreds of dollars. The real people are those that count the pennies. These people are not concerned with what they can get, but more concerned with what they can take.

We live in a new society where, people are slow, like myself to see where things are going. We are slow because we are honest but, there is a new shift taking place and you need to be aware of this shift. You need to open your eyes, just as everyone else has and see that the world is changing.

Nothing can be done to reap the benefits of the wave. Well, let me take that back. Doing nothing will not allow you to reap the benefits of the wave. What are the benefits of the way? Well, the first and foremost is know there is a way and in knowing so, building a passive income, but that's getting ahead of what's in store.

Reading and taking massive action is advised, but asking you to take action now is probably asking you to jump into a living, fire-breathing molten lava volcano. There is no shame in inaction, because the most that will happen because of inaction, is missing the boat. The best that will happen even if you simply took the first step, is providing YOU with a choice.

I love "feel good books" and this is not one of them. Knowledge is power and given most people lack financial choice, the first task of this book has delivered to you as promised. Information. That's correct. You have just been informed about what's really going on as the wave arrives. Your only recourse is to miss the boat or take action.

In review, in this series I have asked that you close your eyes. I have painted a picture of a new wave, a shift in our society where today- you desire more money, but you do not produce anything that generates a passive income. You understand that a wave is on the way and that there are people who actively count pennies and these I call the good people.

And then there are others who I don't talk about much, because these are not so good people who count thousands of dollars in profit. With this new wave in progress, now is your chance to take advantage of the wave. You will not be left behind and you will be counted. Now, let's move on to chapter three.

# CHAPTER 3 – HOW I GENERATED MY GENIE?

My son works with kids. He is an excellent music teacher. Thanks, due in part to his grandfather, he is also talented at woodworking. I never had the tickle to tackle such a tedious task. However, I did have an intentional hand at making sure this happen. When you are poor, and at your disposal are tools and lots of electromechanical broken things in your midst, there is nothing like sitting at the kitchen table or the living room coffee table and teaching young hands how to take apart a clock, a TV, a radio or something electronic, screw by screw, case and all. For children, this is something exciting they can do, as long as the device is not something that is of value and is currently in 100% working order.  Why on earth would I allow my child or your child to take apart something that is working and ask them to put it back together again? Are you crazy! With that out of the way, you need to understand what income is.

What does the word income mean? You and I both know that to live in American with some dignity, we need money to do so. Let me rephrase. To live in this world and in any country, you need money. If you want to live in an apartment, you work therefore earning money, and after taxes, this becomes your income. Now, my objective here is not to get too technical with regards to the fiscal break down of money and how it is derived. The point I want to make is, money earned and is spent so as to afford things you need, things you want and things you desire as well as things that are not good for YOU. Do you feel me?

Some things are necessary, others are not. But to live, you need a form of income. Your skills, your ability to carry out tasks such as cleaning, cooking, writing advertisement copy is something that you do. But, what you truly need is a Genie. You need that proverbial Genie in the bottle that you can go to in dire need to pull from it money when needed. I have asked that from the very beginning to imagine having money when you need it. It is by no means hard, but you must create your own Genie. I asked that you open a savings account. I described in details where and how the bank is to be found and I also told you, that you are by no means obligated to follow this suggestion. However, if you did so- imagine what would happen. What would happen is that you would have your own Genie. Now, most of us already have our own Genie. But what we do not have is a Genie that is producing the money in the bottle. As you continue to read my book, I want you to think and ask yourself about the money aspect of this Genie. Gosh, who is the Genie and why is the Genie so important?

Well, in chapter one I asked a question. What is this book about? Well, over time we learn things about ourselves. We learned things about what an income is, how we give our time away for money. I go on to describe both the good people who count pennies and the not so good people who count the dollars. Now I'm asking you to create a genie. Creating a genie for the purpose of what? So, again why is the Genie so important?

# CHAPTER 4 – WHY REWRITE YOUR INCOME?

Why on earth would I ask you to do something that I would not do myself?

Recall that every year, people make a promise to themselves and to others. We look at ourselves in the mirror and say, I will lose weight as my new year's resolution. Or how about this, I promise I will take better care of myself. Or, something along those lines. But do we? Well, some of us do- BUT for the most part, NO! I can't tell you how many times I quick smoking and I finally did. I had to lose a lot of friends that continue to smoke till this day. They were just a bad influence. It was like being in bed with the wrong crowd of people. Today, I am not associated with people who smoke and have since become vial to the smoke. But this is the thing, I wanted a change. I knew the new wave for which is here already would take advantage of me, so I warn you.

There is this notion that saving money means putting aside money that you would ordinarily spend because by spending very little for the same product or service, it represents the act of saving. By golly, for most people, the art of putting aside money in this fashion is not unordinary. As a matter of fact, I am sure that if you have reached this point in my book without objection that you agree with what I have written here today. Saving money means, not spending it or all of it in exchange for goods and services.

The process of following this method of savings takes patience and a special constitution we call discipline. Additionally, there is the other dreadful aspect of counting the pennies and watching this fortune grow, only for whatever efforts to be wiped away by something called life. Close your eyes. For the next few minutes, imagine you have completed the task of opening your new savings account, depositing the minimum requirement for not incurring a monthly charge for dropping below your minimum deposit. The new accounts representative, asks if you would accept an ATM debit card with your account. Talk about being setup for failure. Do not accept a debit card with or for this account. There is only one reason for not accepting the debit card. Did you know that the easier to access funds, for cash, the faster your plans for failure will occur?" Open your eyes now. Your Genie has been established, but what you fail to understand up to now is, that the Genie is just the guardian of your money. The account is generating income all by itself, but the amount is so small, that only a turtle or ant would appreciate what could be consumed by the interest earned. No, my friend, we are not done with performing the steps for which the Genie can best serve you. For now, it would be in your best interest to continue to read on.

# CHAPTER 5 – IS MONEY AN ANSWER, YES OR NO?

Having funds set aside during this exercise took some time and a great deal of effort on your part. It is very easy to bark orders as the captain of any ship that relies on sails, a rudder, wind and a crew of either men or women. But what is very difficult to do, is to not only bark orders but, perform every single job on the ship while barking orders yourself. Not only is this a good example that demonstrates that no man can perform all of the tasks required to sail a small ship and serve as the captain of their ship. No way, no how. But this also demonstrates the need for a commander and a crew, working together to be sure of a true course that will not steer the ship into the rocks.

Putting aside money is truly an art form and one that should not be taken likely. There are two kinds of people in this world. The first kind are the spenders. There is nothing wrong with spending, especially when spenders feel that tomorrow is just another day for more spending with little expectation that there will not be a next day. The other kind of person is the worrier. The worrier is not a spender. But as a worrier, a great deal of thought and consideration is taken into making the determination of where that next dollar will go. Having multiple savings account give savers a sense of great purpose. Savers have direction and directives. Savers follow patterns of safety and collusion. Their sense of urgency is ensuring that the

Genie is being fed, but in reality- the objective is providing the Genie with a self-sustained income from another source or sources.

As a matter of fact, savers today drive the very same streets which btw have not changed, most can proudly boast they have money in this bank, money in that bank and the like. The pleasure of boasting is now rightfully yours and in your prevue. And there is absolutely nothing wrong with that. From what I recall, was it you or someone else who opened account number two and account number three? Respectfully, the outside forces around you may likely torn down what you are building, creating and destined to inherit. But the bottom line is, your ship is sailing and with the wind on your back, soon your ship will sail far and wide.

By now, I am sure you are wondering thus far, about the merits of the Genie and where this tutorial will take you. I am sure you are being tempted as you follow the directions there in and figure that, I already have a Genie and my Genie is strong and wise. If you feel this way, I understand, but what I have not provided you with today is the formula for ensuring that your Genie survives, fulfills its purpose and become an ever-flowing fountain. A Genie should fulfill your wish and a Genie should withstand destruction, a Genie should be there and available when you need a helping hand.

There is the good and the bad Genie, but today- our focus is on building a foundation for which the Genie can perform for you. Please continue reading because in the next chapter we will talk more about the money.

# CHAPTER 6 – IS THE FREAK SHOW PASSIVE INCOME?

I have stated before and I will state so again, I am not a financial genius. I am not going to bore you with facts, figures and statistics about your decision to open a second or third savings account. I am not going to convince you to take action. You are either going to do so because you want to or you are will not. I am not going to engage in any feel good crap.

If you "want to feel good" about yourself, then read another book that will pump you up, pat you on the back and tell you what good you are doing to yourself and of course after following their instructions, make you "feel like" something is wrong with you.

2017 is the promise year. Upon further examination, if you will recall- in the 80's and 90's the wolves showed themselves openly. Gosh, I wish I could tell you how the Genie I fed which was a charity that took what I fed it month after month, only to become the "but" of bad jokes, thus hurting the real people that the charity was to have helped. Let me go on to say, that when only 20% of what you give actually helps the poor and that my employer encouraged and dam near demanded that thousands of employees give, it was very easy to withdraw my automatic deposit from all charities at that point in time. But, that was another time and if today, a charity asked me for money, I will find the person or a person who truly needed my help and give them my money, right there, right there on the spot. Readers, that Genie died a long time ago. I will never feed that Genie again. I will never build or rather participate in some charity encourage by a company I work for, in such a fashion like that ever again. Never.

2017 is the promise year and the wolves of the previous years who never went to jail, but are now looking at deregulation as a way to fill once again, their pockets with your money are roaming free without fear, without reservation. They are running loose on the streets of every city, of every town of every state. These solves are looking for YOU. Young lads who cling to new and interesting ways to influence money are being held by the hand by these thugs. This all together is a different story, but the fact is- the climate today and moving forward is one that if you pay attention, the story of the past history is about to happen again.

The art of building a business means providing a service of value or a valuable service and selling a good product, or a product that is good. There is no good product or service. Let me explain in further detail. Suppose you are a baker and as a baker, you carefully measure the ingredients you use to make bread. Along the way, after years of baking, you discover that no two loaves of bread are the same, therefore the product is imperfect. Some consumers would never suspect the imperfections of the product, while others who are in fewer numbers would voice their complaints that the bread sold to customer A is different that the bread sold to customer B who is the complainer. Gosh, customer B is an idiot. But customer B does have a valid argument. The bread sold to customer A and B come from the same bowl, and placed in the same oven.

There is no such thing as a perfect "identical" product. Some, would beg the, differ; but again- there is no perfect product. Be the product bread, or a new car. The differences between the productions of products, one from the other are very subtle, but they are there.

The success of building a product is one thing, but the art for asking for the prospects business is another. Getting that money in your hands is the key. I used to write checks and enjoyed that I knew all of the tricks to writing my notes. But today, that is all different and writing checks while old school continues, there is a much more efficient and better way to get cash in your hands. The premise of this conversation is to get the cash into your account, which is the account that the Genie presides for you.

To do so, you will need a PayPal account. What is PayPal? PayPal is simply a way to perform a good or service for anyone on the planet and get paid for said product or service. In other words, PayPal is pay and exchange platform which guarantees the buyer will get what they bought and the seller gets what coming to them. PayPal handles the money transfer between both or all parties. There are many, many other services or platforms out there that operate just as PayPal does. However, all of them have their pros and cons. The biggest plus for using PayPal is the relationship between the money flow of both the buyer and seller. PayPal ensures this integrity and there is no other way to express this relationship. A better way in English would be to say that PayPal is the insurance and policy party. Both parties are ensured by the integrity of the transaction. In the end, all three parties win and that's the bottom line.

The rules of the money collecting party change from time to time and for good reason. The risk is much more on their side than it is on the buyer or the seller's side. To continue to provide the best service possible and to ensure that their interests are addressed, the rules change on occasion. The crooks can and will try to penetrate the deal and for the most part, they always get caught. But, if you can imagine, there are some products that exchange hands that do not fit the bill for using this or that third party. When that happens, the rules must change to take into account of the third parties interest.

At this point in time, we have clearly outlined how funds will be collected and by what means. Every business utilizes some form of collections, else the business would not be in business thus making a profit for whatever products and services are being exchanged for.

## Chapter 7 —Build It Once — Sell It Again & Again?

Congratulations, you have reached the meat of this book. I do not want to bore you with statistics about how to build a financial empire. The numbers associated with building one is staggering, but they are real- in 2017; more so today.

As a matter of fact, this book is directed to you thus making sure that you follow through with objectives of creating accounts that yield income, thus building a business that regenerates.

The Genies objective is to provide you with whatever your needs are, but without this part of the process, all you have is an account that when touched, yields temporary pleasure, and never a choice for solving problems, but no real meat for survival potential for withstanding your additional needs.

You need to build a passive income and this Genie account(s) are going to become the holders of growing wealth, you built once.

Let's begin by saying, "Building a passive income is hard," and for the successful, very rewarding.

The thing you have learned thus far is you need to extend YOU. Your talent is the product. Your knowledge is the product, be it cooking, writing, being organized- you are on the menu. The question becomes- what is the menu item of choice that customers and prospects will see on your menu?

So, take YOU, an idea and turn it into a unique menu options.

Everyone, (such as those that have never done it) will tell you that this step is easy and to be honest, this book series was developed based on an idea. The objective of this book was to change your perception, teach you a few things and to provide a verbal plan that takes you by the hand via no obligation from you to even perform the steps in this book. If you will recall, you are by no means obligated to take these suggestions or perform the steps there in. As a matter of fact, for some of you- this would be considered a good read because there is no financial obligations. But to be fair, you know as well as I that for anyone who wants to change their condition or situation or wealth, you have to make a decision and take action.

So, developing an idea and turning it into something wonderful was the hard part. But what do you invent, what do you think will work for you. What is it that people have done in the past, as a blue print that maybe YOU can follow? The answer to this question is for you to decide. Recall that every year, people think about losing weight- and some people try, others give great lip service and the next year what follows is, those same people doing the same thing all over again. There is absolutely nothing wrong with these people. We are all different, we are who we are and for the most part, people want to be good and have good intentions.

In review, putting all of the pieces together to become what you have in front of you today, was very, very hard. Our objective here is to provide you with several verbal and visual tools. I believe we have done that. I have already introduced you to PayPal. This goes hand in hand with collecting money for services rendered. I have thus far suggested no specific product or service because it is vital that we build for you a visual work flow, a platform to take care of the financial side of building a bank account first. We have a Genie to feed, so let's get with it.

## CHAPTER 8 – SQUEEZE WHAT?

The next part of the process is to introduce you to another piece of technology called a squeeze page. I am 100% sure that you have been exposed to the merits of a squeeze page. I am sure, that you know what a squeeze page is?

But, let me explain for a moment, what has thus been a long road with many twists and turns to a passive income. If you understand correctly, you have thus far accepted that to build a special and lasting income, the first thing needed is an account with a bank. We have also outlined the purpose and scope of the account for which I described as a Genie. Additionally, I have also described in details that for the account to be of great long lasting value, we must fund the account. We do so with an idea product that comes from YOU, your mind. We also understand that to receive compensation for our work, we must utilize a payment processor. Now, with that understanding, we're introduced to the technology called a squeeze page.

What is a squeeze page? In short, a squeeze page is used to capture the prospects information, ie. Name and or email address. This book is not about the merits and theory of a squeeze page. However, when both are put together and the product you build is completed, the end result is your own ATM machine on the outside, and on the inside- a Genie in a bottle.

The product must be simplistic and of value. The best passive income product, is a product that never gets old.

A product that never needs to be revived, re written or one that requires putting lots of money into it to get money out of it.

The best passive income product is a product you make, you setup, you market properly and month after month, it pays you day after day, over and over again. The income goes into your savings account, only to accumulate and grow, to be measured and to one day be spent. Everyone knows what an ATM is? It's a machine that dispenses money.

But let's not go too far into the future there are still things you have to do and be aware of.

Briefly, marketers long ago, learned in the beginning when the internet was formed, that it was very hard to get people to their website. Once it became apparent people were on the website, the next step was to entice people to click a link.

It was during the olden internet days, people were enticed to buy, buy, buy on the internet. People wanted to believe that it was safe, it was wonderful and that it would prove to be the future. Some of what I say here is true and for the most part, there is some safety concerns then yet less risky today and into the future.

Most of the time, the products, and services in the old days were scams. Today, that is not the case because of third party processors that represent both the buyer and the seller, ensuring both parties are 100% satisfied. Now, what is 100% satisfaction?

Please understand that there is no perfect product. If you look past the perfection, that is the beauty of the internet today. The buying and selling aspects are invisible, fast and rewarding. Have you ever looked at garments you purchase, cars you drive or sandwiches you eat. This book is probably the best example or imperfection. No, every now and again, I will create a typo and not say, something that could be said better or maybe left out. People who want something to be perfect and are in the business of running a business, are less likely to be successful. You do what you can and you can do what you want. But no one is perfect. No one thing is perfect and there is no assembly line that can product a product with such precision that each widget is the same. Sorry, but everything, everyone and every person is different.

Parties today, are less likely to be scammed today!  You need a squeeze page to capture the email address of your visitor, so you can market to them once they leave your website, whether they prospect or customer, buy today or not. I love the phrase, "what's in it for me"?

What's in it for me is, the ability to also encourage visitors to buy another product you might suggest, develop or create out of thin air.

Rather than have success with one purchase, you could enjoy success multiple purchases over a period of time.

Yes, you want to earn money, again and again.

And you can collect that money very easily, also.

Just promise and deliver. Promise and deliver. Again, promise and deliver.

Close your eyes, "Book publishing is very hard work, but the rewards are very satisfactory. For some people, the art of publishing requires not just hard work, a good work ethic, luck and a changed mindset.

For some people, no matter what they touch, it turns into a best seller. That is your goal. Turnout a best seller.

That is your product. That is the point. Become a best seller of YOU.

Now, within a few months, that can happen for you. Hard work and a bit of luck and there you have it-the product. The book is your best seller." You can open your eyes now.

Take a few minutes and think about writing a book, think about developing a product that people will enjoy and love. If you can't think of a product, then take "YOU", your passion and bundle it up.

Think about giving value to the reader, your customer, your prospect, the world.

Simply, *think about that book inside of you*. Everyone has a book inside them. Sometimes the book is easy to draw to the surface, other times the book is so darn hard to materialize. I know, because it happened to me.

But bottom line, *we all have something to say to the world* and now or today is your chance to think about your message. Write your message into a book.

Say something true or say something meaningful and understand, there are listeners out there. "Close your eyes and try it!" You will be pleasantly surprised.

You do not need to be a professor of English something or another. What you need are three things. You need an idea, you need action and you need, the right frame of mind. I hope you enjoyed this book. I am by no means a Mr. Ramsey or a Mr. Kiyosaki, but I do have a message to tell the world which was delivered to me and the words flew from my fingers into the computer keyboard. I am so sorry, what I am describing is finger painting. But honestly folks, this entire "Close Your Eyes" series was dreamed up to provide the world with value, demonstrating how we all need to feed our Genie and thank you for feeding mine.

# Chapter 9 - Building An Email List

## Sequential Email List Building

Building an email list is hard. Let me rephrase, building an email list is hard work. It requires that you understand who will be giving their email address to you. So, please understand when I say that, if anyone tells you that it is NOT hard, they are a liar.

To build a passive income, a mailing list is vital as well as an automated system of taking orders, delivering what was promised (all without lifting a figure) and automatically.

Our Genie, will need to build an email list. The beauty of any system that makes money is automating the tasks involved once and spinning the (blueprint), in any niche. What is a niche? A niche is a subject matter that interests YOU, this is unique, special and for the most part- your parade. For example, if your talent is cooking and you love cooking deserts. Then your niche is "cooking deserts". You could probably write about your niche all day long. Now, some people would call cooking a niche. Well, in the broader since, "Cooking" is at the top of the niche. We waddle down the "niche" and specialize, thus creating and settling on a sub niche.

Now that I have explained what a niche is, we need to focus on building an email list. Let's start by looking at the email building niche. There are five simple email messages. Each message when added to an autoresponder will send as program on a daily, weekly or twice a day basis to a prospect.

Once the prospect provides their email address, a report is delivered to the prospect and the prospect is added to another list. On this "new list" prospects are sent more information on occasion, but later in the email sequence the prospects are sent to a sales page. The sales page is where we actually send our offer which results in our prospect becoming a customer. The customer is then added to a new email list, called a buyers list. The buyers list is very valuable. This is of customer is valuable because you have provided these buyers with something they wanted and they are most likely to purchase from you again. Let's continue our discussion with building an email sequence. **Here are (5) example email message that you can use to model five or more emails for your niche.**

These drip fed emails are sent to prospects over a course of 5 days. You will have to design your own email messages or you can purchase drip email messages for use with your autoresponder. To draft an email message, use the follow formula:

Salutation: Hi, Howdy, Frank

❖ Subject: Say what you think

❖ Call to Action: Click here! Download Now!

❖ More information – Always provide value

❖ Close – Call to action!

**Very Important:** Be natural, do not over complicate this process and tell your prospect what you want them to do. In each email message, I am telling the prospect what to do to receive more information and of course, I provide a link for my free report.

Speak to your prospect in your natural voice. If you are familiar with Dear John letter, then your email message should be much more upbeat and enticing.

How often should you email your prospect? A: Once you understand the process, you can email as often as you like. Your customer can always unsubscribe from your list, but if you have a close relationship with your prospects, then you will want to respect their privacy, so use you judgement.

You can add value to your email by adding information in the form of a story. Tell your prospect at the top of your email message (the beginning) what you were doing before you sat down to write this email message. Maybe you learned something on YouTube and the information could be of use to your prospect. Tell the prospect about your findings. Maybe you read a book and found a specific chapter that you found interesting or maybe you like what the author said and decided to quote them. Do so in your email message sequence. The objective is to provide value, humanize yourself and being a real person and add value by educating and giving away tips, tricks etc. You can create an email drip feed within an hour. Here is a trick that I use. Go to your yahoo news and read the headlines.

Use these headlines as the subject to your emails, but modify the headline to make your subject better and of course more like you. Here is an example. I was on google news and the head line reads. "Alaska man survives brown bear attack thanks to quick-thinking friend". Your subject like might ready, "Quick thinking leads to huge email profits". This one came from the top of my head and the thing about this new subject is, it is perfect. Here is another one "Diagnose & Fix Windows". I would use the subject: Diagnose and Fix Your Mailing List. Do you see how that works? There are hundreds of news story headlines you can use. Write the subject titles like you were talking with a friend, whom you met for the second or third time.

You just know what to say and not to say to someone whom you have met a few times and you are just talking about this or that. Nothing special, nothing obscure and nothing nasty.

Take a look at the crafted email message below and let's move on to Sales Page, theory and operation or as some people like to call it- the rain maker.

**-Day-1**

Subject: *Visualize Huge Profits Online*

John Here!

Want to Rocket Launch building an
Incredible list of buying customers?

Want to learn how to build a killer Mailing list fast!

And finally, do you want to learn the secrets of
successfully building a list?

If you answered YES - then...

The steps are easy, the results are fast!

**Click here – Free Report**

This free report will teach!

Tell you what you need to know and fast!

If anyone told you that building a list was easy, then run
fast.

Building a list is not easy, but this report will certainly
reveal what works and what does not work.


**Click here – Free Report**

**-Day 2-**

Subject: *Build Me A List*

What's this I hear.... about list building?

But first...

*Click Here – Free Report*

I have a question for you..

It's a serious question.

You see how I sent you this email.

You're on my email list.

I'm sending YOU emails about all sorts of things, from trainings, tools, tricks, and ways to improve your online business.

But did you know that emails like this are a HUGE part of my online business?

In fact, OVER 95% of online marketers use this method as one of the #1 way to profit online.

*Click Here – Free Report*

Don't wait! Get this! No Autoresponder required!

**-Day 3-**

Subject: ***You can do anything!***

You can become anything you want, but what if you could attract hundreds of people with a mailing list.

All you have to do is just get started by using this free report.

Everything that you need is right here.

It's all listed right HERE!

***Click Here – Free Report***

If you've ever thought about having your own email list, this IS one email list you have to sign up for!

***Click Here – Free Report***

Check it out today!

You will be glad you did!

Don't wait! Get this! No Autoresponder required!

**-Day 4-**

Subject: ***Why can he do it but I can't?***

Don't ever let Billy tell you, that you are worthless and cannot think for yourself.

You can become anything you want!

I know that it is hard building a mailing list and once you have one, the money is in the list.

But first, you have to understand all of the methods used for building a list. Most of the methods are worth lots of money because they do work. But then, there are other methods that do not work as well or effectively as one would like.

I build my list based on my experience and because my lists are so effective, I decided to share my experience with anyone for free.

It's all listed right HERE!

***Click Here – Free Report***

Building a list is not easy if you do not have the knowledge to make it easier.

***Click Here – Free Report***

Check it out today! You will be glad you did!

Don't wait! Get this! No Autoresponder required!

**-Day 5-**

Subject: *The Mailing List Report*

Hi

Today, is the last day that I am offering my free list building report.

But, let me ask you.

Have you tried to build a list? Did you use an autoresponder?

Was your squeeze page converting? Did your traffic ever convert? If you answered no to a few of these questions, then you need my report.

In my report I outline what you need, where to get and how to attract your prospects. I make building a list easy and you will get results.

*Click Here – Free Report*

Check it out today! You will be glad you did!

Don't wait! Get this! No Autoresponder required!

I always put in a bonus in my reports to provide added value and my readers enjoy the extra's I add.

*Click Here – Free Report*

## CHAPTER 10 – THE RAIN MAKER

What the heck is a rain maker (sales page)? A sales page is used to introduce your product offering and make THE SALE. The Sales Page makes the sale by offering as many benefits and demystify reasonable objections leading to read to the final decision, of Yes! I want to purchase that product NOW!

The Genie needs to be fed and the way to do it is with this money rain maker. Your sales page consist of a product name and head line. It's obvious that you will want to include your product name at the top. Here is a good example. Suppose your product is a book cover generator. You will want to describe your products attributes. How easy it is, how powerful it is. What it can do and why YOU need the product and such. You can include graphics, a slew of attributes such as training, how easy it is to use, features, how it will save you money and more. But at the very end of your sales page after giving your potential customer all the information they need to make a buying decision, at the bottom of the sales page is a button to click Buy It. In some cases, there is a try-it button for those who are on the fence.

Now, this book is not about to demonstrate for you how to build a sales page, but rather describe what a sales page is and what your sales page should have on it. The rain maker is the last step in the process and once your prospect clicks the buy button, they will have become-your customer. That's right, your customer is added to the buyers list and now it's time to deliver what your customer purchased. Your thank you page not only collects the rain, but it also delivers the product to your customer. Now, in this example I used a book cover generator.

The product could be a valuable book, a report or something of that nature that can be delivered via email or via a download link. Delivery of the product is strictly up to you. I prefer to delivery my products via Gum Road. Would you be interested in my offers? Let's see. What do we have here?

# DESIGNING YOUR OWN SPECIAL LABEL PRODUCTS

After writing this book, I decided to add some additional value by giving your examples of products that I sell. Yes, I preach what I write. Here goes:

## Turbo List Builder

What is Turbo List Builder? In a nut shell, this product makes building a list very easy, because of the many different designs and such. You will most likely find more information, videos on YouTube. But because this product is highly used by this publisher, support is provide when you purchase here.

Turbo List Builder - https://gum.co/oEkgr

## Site Spinner

One of my passions is taking a problem and designing a solution. Site Spinner is sold on eBay for less than $20. The software is used to create webpages in a "what you see is what you get" design. Well, the help file system is excellent in that you can find mostly everything you need about designing a "fill in the form" web pages.

The product makes it very easy to just sit back and design your website. The problem is, simply taking the code and making a squeeze page or sales page design that you really, really like and integrating the two, so you have ALL the control you need to be as creative as you want. I worked on the problem for about a week and solicited the help of a programmer on fiverr.

It worked out that the code I have in this product can be integrated into all designs that are written in html. What does this all mean? There are five lines of code that can be integrated into any squeeze page you want to use as a sample that will work with Site Spinner GUI software. The following gem will save you time, enabling you to model (not copy) any squeeze page! Plus you learn PHP.

Learn PHP | SS Squeeze Page - https://gum.co/tJUAQ

There are just a few of the products that I sell to supplement my income and I would encourage you to do the same. I have done my very best to make the very best product that I can to my ability and I hope that you have enjoyed this book.

I apologize today, if there are miss spelled words or incomplete sentences. If you would be so kind as to bring them to my attention by writing me at info@zorbobook.com, I would really appreciate it if you would join my mailing list.

Q: The #1 Reason people failed to start an online business.
A: Perfection, Fear, Not knowing how.

Don't let Fear, Perfection and knowledge stop you! Read as many books as you can to help you understand and invest in products that offer a money back guarantee, in this way you will have less fear in trying a product. Additionally, look at your attempt as a journey to success when you can look back and say to your audience, what you did, how you felt and that aha moment when things started to change for you.

## Can I Ask A Favor?

If you enjoyed this book, found it useful or otherwise then I'd really appreciate it if you would post a short review on Amazon. I do read all the reviews personally so that I can continually write what people are wanting. Be sure to click the link *above* for our other titles.

Thanks for your support!